Krazy For

Kittens

2025 Calendar

JANUARY 2025

SUNDAY	MONDAY	TUESDAY	WEDNESDAY	THURSDAY	FRIDAY	SATURDAY
29	30	31	1	2	3	4
5	6	7	8	9	10	11
12	13	14	15	16	17	18
19	20	21	22	23	24	25
26	27	28	29	30	31	1

FEBRUARY 2025

SUNDAY	MONDAY	TUESDAY	WEDNESDAY	THURSDAY	FRIDAY	SATURDAY
26	27	28	29	30	31	1
2	3	4	5	6	7	8
9	10	11	12	13	14	15
16	17	18	19	20	21	22
23	24	25	26	27	28	1

MARCH 2025

SUNDAY	MONDAY	TUESDAY	WEDNESDAY	THURSDAY	FRIDAY	SATURDAY
23	24	25	26	27	28	1
2	3	4	5	6	7	8
9	10	11	12	13	14	15
16	17	18	19	20	21	22
23 / 30	24 / 31	25	26	27	28	29

APRIL 2025

SUNDAY	MONDAY	TUESDAY	WEDNESDAY	THURSDAY	FRIDAY	SATURDAY
30	31	1	2	3	4	5
6	7	8	9	10	11	12
13	14	15	16	17	18	19
20	21	22	23	24	25	26
27	28	29	30	1	2	3

MAY 2025

SUNDAY	MONDAY	TUESDAY	WEDNESDAY	THURSDAY	FRIDAY	SATURDAY
27	28	29	30	1	2	3
4	5	6	7	8	9	10
11	12	13	14	15	16	17
18	19	20	21	22	23	24
25	26	27	28	29	30	31

JUNE 2025

SUNDAY	MONDAY	TUESDAY	WEDNESDAY	THURSDAY	FRIDAY	SATURDAY
1	2	3	4	5	6	7
8	9	10	11	12	13	14
15	16	17	18	19	20	21
22	23	24	25	26	27	28
29	30	1	2	3	4	5

JULY 2025

SUNDAY	MONDAY	TUESDAY	WEDNESDAY	THURSDAY	FRIDAY	SATURDAY
29	30	1	2	3	4	5
6	7	8	9	10	11	12
13	14	15	16	17	18	19
20	21	22	23	24	25	26
27	28	29	30	31	1	2

AUGUST 2025

SUNDAY	MONDAY	TUESDAY	WEDNESDAY	THURSDAY	FRIDAY	SATURDAY
27	28	29	30	31	1	2
3	4	5	6	7	8	9
10	11	12	13	14	15	16
17	18	19	20	21	22	23
24 / 31	25	26	27	28	29	30

SEPTEMBER 2025

SUNDAY	MONDAY	TUESDAY	WEDNESDAY	THURSDAY	FRIDAY	SATURDAY
31	1	2	3	4	5	6
7	8	9	10	11	12	13
14	15	16	17	18	19	20
21	22	23	24	25	26	27
28	29	30	1	2	3	4

OCTOBER 2025

SUNDAY	MONDAY	TUESDAY	WEDNESDAY	THURSDAY	FRIDAY	SATURDAY
28	29	30	1	2	3	4
5	6	7	8	9	10	11
12	13	14	15	16	17	18
19	20	21	22	23	24	25
26	27	28	29	30	31	1

NOVEMBER 2025

SUNDAY	MONDAY	TUESDAY	WEDNESDAY	THURSDAY	FRIDAY	SATURDAY
26	27	28	29	30	31	1
2	3	4	5	6	7	8
9	10	11	12	13	14	15
16	17	18	19	20	21	22
23 / 30	24	25	26	27	28	29

DECEMBER 2025

SUNDAY	MONDAY	TUESDAY	WEDNESDAY	THURSDAY	FRIDAY	SATURDAY
30	1	2	3	4	5	6
7	8	9	10	11	12	13
14	15	16	17	18	19	20
21	22	23	24	25	26	27
28	29	30	31	1	2	3

The Top 30 Cat Breeds

Abyssinian
American Bobtail
American Curl
American Shorthair
American Wirehair
Balinese
Bengal
Birman
Bombay
British Shorthair
Burmese
Chartreux
Cornish Rex
Devon Rex
Egyptian Mau
Exotic Shorthair
Havana Brown
Himalayan
Japanese Bobtail
Khao Manee
Maine Coon
Manx
Norwegian Forest Cat
Ocicat
Oriental Shorthair
Persian
Ragdoll
Russian Blue
Scottish Fold
Siamese

How to Train a Cat to Use the Toilet

Training a cat to use the toilet instead of a litter box can be done, though it requires patience and consistency. Here's a step-by-step guide to help you toilet-train your cat:

1. Start by moving the litter box
Gradual location change: Move the litter box closer to the bathroom. Over time, place it next to the toilet.
Raise the height: Gradually elevate the litter box by placing it on a stack of newspapers or books. The goal is to get the cat comfortable jumping up and using the litter box at the same height as the toilet seat.
2. Transition to the toilet
Place the litter box on the toilet: Once the litter box is at toilet height, place it directly on the toilet seat. This helps your cat associate the toilet as the new place for elimination.
Use a training kit or make-shift seat: Special cat toilet training kits like "Litter Kwitter" or "CitiKitty" are available. These kits come with an insert that fits inside the toilet bowl. If you don't have a kit, you can create a temporary solution with a wide, sturdy metal bowl or a pie tin, filling it with a small amount of litter.
3. Introduce the toilet itself
Start with a small hole: If you're using a training kit, the insert will have different stages where you progressively widen the hole in the center to simulate the toilet bowl. If you're improvising, gradually reduce the amount of litter while making a small hole in the center of your temporary device.
Increase the hole size: Over time, enlarge the hole so your cat eventually eliminates directly into the water below.
Remove the device: After your cat successfully uses the toilet with a larger hole, you can remove the training device altogether.
4. Reinforce good behavior
Positive reinforcement: Reward your cat with praise and treats after they successfully use the toilet.
Monitor for stress: Keep an eye on your cat to ensure they aren't stressed or reverting to inappropriate elimination elsewhere.
Tips for Success:
Patience: The process can take several weeks, or even months, depending on your cat's personality and adaptability.
Slow transitions: Don't rush the process. Each step can take several days to weeks before your cat is fully comfortable.
Hygiene: Keep the toilet seat clean and accessible. You'll need to train yourself to leave the seat up and lid down, as your cat needs access to the bowl.
Important Considerations:
Not all cats adapt well: Some cats may never take to toilet training. Stress or accidents may increase if they don't feel comfortable.
Toilet lids: Ensure your cat can still access the toilet by leaving the lid up. Otherwise, you may need to retrain them.

www.ingramcontent.com/pod-product-compliance
Lightning Source LLC
Chambersburg PA
CBHW061147030426
42335CB00002B/138
9781959209324